North Dart pub walks

Robert Hesketh

Bossiney Books

This corrected reprint 2011
First published 2006 by
Bossiney Books Ltd, 33 Queens Drive, Ilkley, LS29 9QW
www.bossineybooks.com

© 2006 Robert Hesketh   All rights reserved
ISBN 978-1-899383-83-2

Acknowledgements
The maps are by Graham Hallowell
Cover based on a design by Heards Design Partnership
Photographs are by the author or from the publishers' own collection

Printed in Great Britain by R Booth Ltd, Penryn, Cornwall

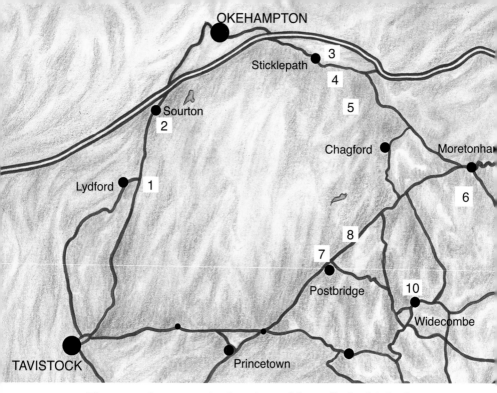

The approximate starting locations of the walks in this book

Introduction

Higher and wilder than anywhere else in southern England, Dartmoor is a place of stark beauty. Each granite tor has its own profile and the Dartmoor pony is a breed apart, but it is the mark of man more than anything else which gives Dartmoor its unique character and its exceptional interest. Much of it can only be discovered on foot or horseback.

This is England's richest prehistoric landscape: stone rows, circles, pounds and field boundaries, the foundations of houses and hilltop burial chambers abound. Several of the best are included in these walks, along with medieval longhouses and ancient routes still served by clapper bridges and marked by granite crosses. We visit tin-streaming sites, mines and leats, souvenirs of Dartmoor's once rich but now vanished industry, as well as a water-powered edge-tool factory and several historic churches.

Dartmoor also has some excellent pubs; each walk includes at least one. Please note that several are family-run businesses and may close one or two days a week, especially outside the high season. Check first!

At 14km (9 miles) or less, all the routes in this book can be walked in a day, some in a morning or afternoon. Start with the shorter walks if you are out of practice. The time you need depends on how fast you walk and how interested you are in what you see; each walk has several extras, from prehistoric monuments to historic churches, and the approximate times given do not allow for the time you might want to spend exploring these.

Safety (please take seriously)

Walking Dartmoor is safe and trouble free – if you are prepared. In the first place, the weather can change suddenly. High winds, sudden temperature drops, fogs and driving rain can all be par for the course, even in summer.

Please do not go without good walking boots and suitable clothing. Drinking water, map and compass, plus waterproofs and an extra layer are essential, as well as a comfortable rucksack. Many, including me, add to the list a walking stick, mobile phone (though reception is patchy) and food. Lock your car and don't leave valuables in it.

The sketch maps in this book are just that – sketches. You should go equipped with the Ordnance Survey 'Explorer OL28'.

Ticks are a potential nuisance, especially in hot, humid weather. Wearing long trousers and socks offers some protection against these tiny parasites, which can carry a viral infection, Lyme disease. If one does attach itself to you, remove it promptly and carefully with tweezers, being careful to leave none of it in your skin.

None of the walks in this book enter the military firing ranges, marked by red and white posts. Be careful never to enter these areas without having first checked firing times on (0800) 458 4868.

Access

Unenclosed moorland areas are generally open access. Please keep to paths over enclosed moorland, use and close gates as appropriate and keep dogs under control.

More information about Dartmoor

There is too little space in this book to explain fully what you are seeing. The following books will be helpful if you are new to the moor:

High Dartmoor – a shortish guide, Robert Hesketh
Ancient Dartmoor, Paul White
Medieval Dartmoor, Paul White

I am sure you will enjoy these walks as I have.

Robert Hesketh

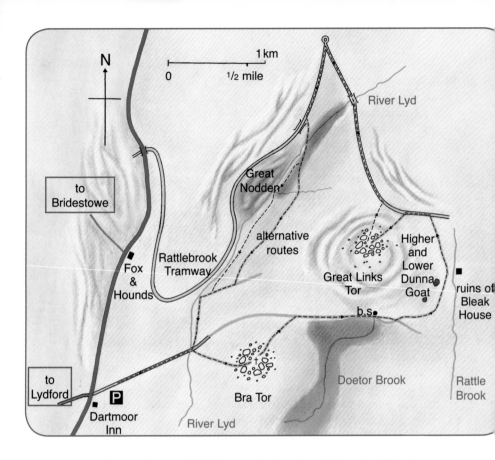

Walk 1 Great Links Tor and the Castle Inn, Lydford

Distance: 13 km (8 miles)   Time: 4¹/₂ hours
Character: Two steep ascents are rewarded with wonderful views.
Allow time to explore the interesting industrial remains from tinning
and peat cutting. Much of the route is on open moorland – wet after
rain. Map, compass and boots essential.

Start from the car park at SX 525854. This is 300 m up a rough track
by the Dartmoor Inn on the A386, opposite the turning to Lydford.
The car park is just beyond the first gate.

Follow the track ahead from the car park, keeping the stone wall on
your left. An impressive line of tors faces you. Cross the infant River
Lyd by stepping stones. Head east up the flank of Bra Tor – also
known locally as Brat Tor or Brattor, and given as Bray Tor on the OS
map – by the rough path, aiming for the granite cross on the summit.
William Widgery, the local landscape painter, erected it in 1887 to celebrate Queen Victoria's Golden Jubilee.

4

Walk north-east from Brat Tor for 750 m, following a faint path over the turf until you strike a distinct west-east path. Turn right onto this old tinners' track, worn deep into the ground in places like a trench. The extensive overgrown workings to the south, especially around the head of Doetor Brook, give a vivid idea of how much rock Dartmoor tinners moved, mostly using hand tools in the pre-industrial age. Follow the track east, ignoring side turnings.

The treeless windswept beauty of the high moor opens out in front. Look out for a characteristic Dartmoor boundary stone ('BS' on OS maps) inscribed L for Lydford parish and BS for Bridestowe on its opposite face. About 150 m beyond this, make sure you keep left on the track which heads east, not ESE.

When you are abreast of Lower Dunna Goat, bear left. (If you reach the firing range marker poles you've gone too far! These warn walkers to go no further when the red flags are flying.) Follow the path NNE with two small tors, Lower and then Higher Dunna Goat, on your left. Across Rattle Brook from Higher Dunna Goat is the aptly named ruin, Bleak House, the lonely home of the West of England Compressed Peat Company's representatives. Six companies tried to make a success of digging peat here between 1868 and 1955. They scarred the land, but time has healed the wounds.

Walk towards the ruin, but don't cross the stream. Keep left along the top of the left bank, then follow a distinct track heading sometimes north, sometimes north-west.

When you meet the Rattlebrook Railway, turn left. The rails have gone, but the cuttings, embankments and bridges remain. It was built to join the LSWR line running from Okehampton to Plymouth, which is now, west of Meldon Quarry, a cycle route.

Just beyond the summit point, a peaty track leads up the left bank of the cutting. This allows you to detour to visit Great Links Tor, an impressive granite pile which is one of the highest points of Dartmoor and, at 586 m (over 1900 ft), almost qualifies as a mountain. It offers even finer views than Bra Tor. Return to the tramway and turn left.

Walk downhill for nearly 2 km, then turn sharp left where the trucks used to stop and reverse down the next section. Continue till you come to a bridge, at which point bear left on a rather indistinct path heading south. Follow it down and cross the River Lyd, then turn right along the east bank. There is no defined path near the river, so pick your way carefully through the old tin stream workings. Alternatively, there's a slightly easier route higher up the hill – see sketch map. Great Nodden rises on the right, forming a small gorge. Composed of shale, it marks the boundary between moorland granite and metamorphic rocks to the west.

Recross the river by the stepping stones used at the start and retrace your steps to the car park. You now have a rich choice of pubs. The Dartmoor Inn lies at the end of the track. My publisher swears by the Fox and Hounds, 1.5 km towards Okehampton, but my own preference is the Castle Inn in Lydford itself, a mile ahead.

The Castle Inn, Lydford
01822 820241

Built in the 16th century, the Castle Inn was originally the home of the keeper of Lydford Castle. It served as a farmhouse, and later as an ale house too. It has many interesting features including three open fires: the one in the restaurant is medieval and was taken from Lydford Castle itself. There are exposed beams (some ancient) and slate floors.

Of particular interest are the Saxon pennies on display. These were minted between the reigns of Edward the Martyr (975-8) and Edward the Confessor (1042-66) at Lydford, when it was one of four mints in Devon – the others being at Totnes, Exeter and Barnstaple. Many early English coins, some looted by the Vikings, others paid to them as Dane geld, are now housed in Scandinavian museums. It is some satisfaction to know that our ancestors beat off the Danes at Lydford in 997. This is commemorated by a plaque near the church.

Walk 2   Sourton and Meldon

Distance: 10.8 km (6³/4 miles)   Time: 3¹/2 hours
Character: The climb to Sourton Tor (440 m) is rewarded by
tremendous views of north Dartmoor and on to the north coast and
Bodmin Moor. En route, there is a Victorian ice works, a handsome
reservoir, and a worm's eye view of a viaduct. Map and compass are
essential: choose a clear day. We end at a unique inn.

The Highwayman at Sourton (01837 861243)
The building has a medieval core and later became a coaching inn. In
1961 its transformation began into something rich and strange. It is
packed with bizarre and imaginative detail.

You enter by the stagecoach lobby, formed out of one of the original
coaches used on the Okehampton-Launceston road, and head for the
bar, made of Dartmoor bog oak. There is a door from a whaling ship
and a grotto full of stuffed animals. Church pews, cartwheels, lanterns,
Old Mother Hubbard's shoe and sewing machines all feature, along
with a host of eccentric items.

Drive 50 m up the lane opposite the Highwayman (signed BRIDLE-
PATH TO THE MOOR) and park by the village hall, at SX 535903. Walk
back towards the inn to see a stone incised with a cross and the letters
OXO. It is a 10th century Christian stone, but erected here in 1985.

Retrace your steps and walk on, to Sourton church. This has a good,
typically Devonian, wagon roof, Charles II's coat-of-arms and a lancet
window with medieval stained glass. Follow the bridlepath over the

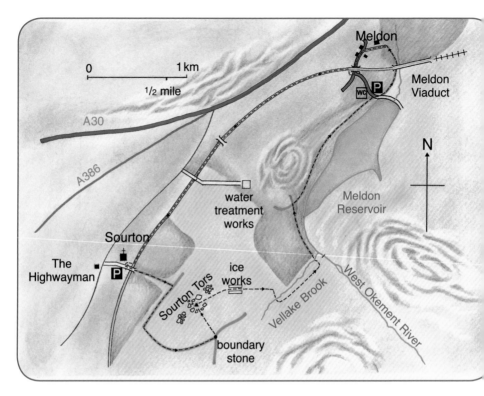

railway bridge. Take the left fork (WEST DEVON WAY) and head up onto the open moor.

At a junction of tracks, turn right and walk on beneath the stern ridge of Sourton Tors: keep fairly close to the wall on your right. Walk past a narrow wooden gate, then bear left and onto a clear track heading uphill, initially SE then E. This soon becomes an old cart track.

The views open out as you gain height, heading between Sourton Tors on the left and a deep combe on the right. Lake Viaduct is particularly dramatic. Stop at a path junction, where the small boundary stone (BS on the Ordnance Survey map) is marked B, SO and O, for Bridestowe, Sourton and Okehampton parishes.

Now head NNW to a triangulation pillar. The heights of Bodmin Moor are outlined on the western horizon, north-west lies the coast, behind you is a superb view of Corn Ridge and Yes Tor. From the tor, walk NE and downhill to the grassy mounds and trenches which are the remnants of Sourton Ice Works.

The site was chosen in 1875 because it is particularly cold, and there was a good spring from which water was piped to the trenches, where it froze in winter. The ice was cut and stored in insulated chambers. In

summer, the blocks were cut again and transported to Plymouth's fish market by horse and cart.

From the ice works head due east to meet a path parallel to a stone wall crowned with a post-and-wire fence. Follow this path as it diverges away from the wall to cross Vellake Brook near its head. Take the rough path on the far side of the brook and follow it NE for 700 m. Opposite a weir, the path descends steeply left to cross Vellake Brook then passes through a wooden gate. Enter RESERVOIR WALK FOR MELDON CAR PARK. Walk ahead, with the west Okement on your right, to a crossing of paths. Turn right through a gate (RESERVOIR WALK FOR MELDON CAR PARK).

Reaching the lane which leads to the dam, continue ahead TO MELDON VIADUCT (incidentally, there are public toilets in the car park, just out of your view). The path dips to the river. Keep to the left bank, past a lake (a former quarry) and a disused limekiln, to walk under Meldon Viaduct. This was built for the London & South Western Railway, with a span of 167 m and a maximum height of 36 m. Constructed in wrought iron for single line working in 1874, it was doubled in steel for two line operation in 1879.

Follow the track up to Meldon Farm. Walk on past the farm to the lane. Turn left, uphill. Walk under the bridge and turn right to join the cycle path – the former railway. Turn left onto the path, SOURTON.

Continue for 3 km to Sourton church, and retrace your steps to the Highwayman.

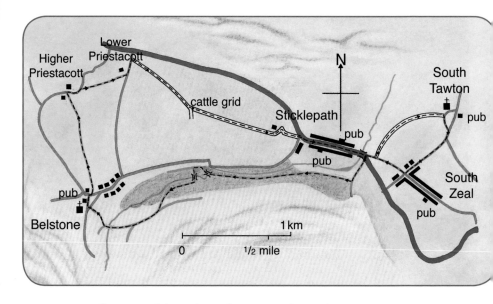

Walk 3   Sticklepath, Belstone and South Tawton

Length: 10 km (6 1/4 miles)   Time: 3 hours
Character: Mainly a riverside and field path walk, this route is full
of interest. Finch Foundry has working waterwheels driving various
machinery. South Tawton has a handsome church and church house.
This is a walk with no less than four pubs – one at either end of a
figure-of-eight and two in the middle!
   Do not attempt the walk if the river is in flood.

Park in Sticklepath's main street, near the Finch Foundry (National Trust). This 19th century forge and edge-tool factory, powered by three waterwheels fed by a leat from the River Taw, is now a working museum. There are regular demonstrations of the machinery, including a grindstone, drop hammer and tilt hammer. At the rear is an unusual Quaker burying ground, recalling the early Quaker community in Sticklepath and the welcome they gave the Wesleys on their journeys westwards. Walk downhill past the Taw River Inn with its 17th century date-stones.

   Cross the bridge, noting its milestone, and turn right onto PUBLIC BRIDLEPATH THE MOOR etc. Follow the path alongside the river, passing a footbridge, and go through a gate. Turn right, PUBLIC FOOTPATH SKAIGH. Walk on the bankside path past the old mill and the sluice gate feeding the leat for Finch Foundry. The path winds through mixed deciduous woodland, accompanied by the river's music. Moss and ferns grow thickly, testifying to the clean moist air.

10

Cross a footbridge carved with a quotation from *Tarka the Otter*. (In the novel, Tarka disputes a rabbit with Swagdagger the stoat.) Bear right out to a track and turn left (BELSTONE). Follow the track for 100m then turn left to recross the river by the next footbridge. Turn right for BELSTONE and keep to the path parallel to the river.

The path rises slightly and joins another path. After a while keep right and right again, to recross the Taw again via a footbridge just to the left of a ford. Keep right and steeply uphill, to enjoy a fine view of Belstone Cleave, reminiscent of Lustleigh Cleave (Walk 9).

Head for the centre of the village, dignified by its medieval church tower, and pass The Tors. This is first recorded as the New Inn in 1815, burned down and was replaced by the present building in 1896. Walk ahead to Zion Chapel – prominently labelled TELEGRAPH OFFICE. Turn right and after 30m turn left, PUBLIC FOOTPATH.

Keep the hedge on your right through two fields, then continue with the hedge on your left. Cross a stile and walk ahead as signed through a series of small fields, stiles and gates to a tarred lane. Turn right by Lower Priestacott.

Follow the lane for 220m. Take the second footpath on the right, TONGUE END. Cross three fields to a lane (just to the right of the pumping station). Turn left, and after 125m turn right, PUBLIC BRIDLE-PATH SKAIGH AND STICKLEPATH. This old track, once the main

11

highway from Okehampton, offers views onto Dartmoor and over the rolling hills of mid-Devon to Exmoor.

At a cattle grid keep left. At the end of the old track carry straight on down the main street, passing (or entering) the Devonshire Inn. Retrace your steps past the foundry and over the bridge. Fork left and after 50 m turn left (TARKA TRAIL). Follow this pleasant green lane uphill. The tall granite tower of St Andrew's church, South Tawton, appears as you top the hill: it has fine carved altar rails and pulpit.

Leave by the lychgate, where the church, village square, and 16th century church house, with its large granite blocks and external stairs, make an attractive group. Walk ahead passing the Seven Stars to your left. Keep right (SOUTH ZEAL) at the stump of Moon's Cross, which directed travellers from North Devon to fork left for eastern Dartmoor or right for the west.

After 500 m, at Zeal Head Cross, turn right again for Sticklepath and retrace your steps up from the bridge.

The Devonshire Inn (01837 840626)
Intriguing and unspoilt, this is a 16th century thatched inn on the old Exeter road. Beer is cooled by water from the leat and customers are warmed by hearty log fires. Take time to explore the bar, parlour and snug. There are many curiosities including flintlock weapons, bread ovens, a ship's bell, a sea chest and a grandfather clock. The Inn has customer car parking, and serves food at lunchtimes.

Walk 4   South Zeal and Cosdon Beacon

Distance: 12.5 km (7 3/4 miles)   Time: 4 hours
Character: Choose a clear day: the panoramic views of Dartmoor,
mid-Devon and Exmoor are superb. The prehistoric stone circle and
triple stone row should not be missed. Most of the route is on open
moor: parts will be wet after rain. Map, compass and navigational
skills are essential. This is a fairly demanding walk.

The Oxenham Arms (01837) 840244

A handsome granite and thatch building, the inn bears the arms of the
Oxenhams on the sign. Said to have been built in the 12th century, it
was recorded as an inn in 1477. Later it was rebuilt as the dower house
of the Burgoynes and then the Oxenhams. The snug contains a granite
menhir, perhaps 5000 years old. There are many other features,
including oak doors and beams and original flagstones.

Park at South Zeal's free car park (SX 652934). Turn right out of the
car park, up the lane. Fork right at 'Oakfield', by the smithy. Walk up
to the main road (formerly the A30), cross and walk up BRIDLEPATH
TO THE MOOR.

After 170 m, cut out a dog-leg in the track by using the short cut
(PATH). When the track forks, keep right.

13

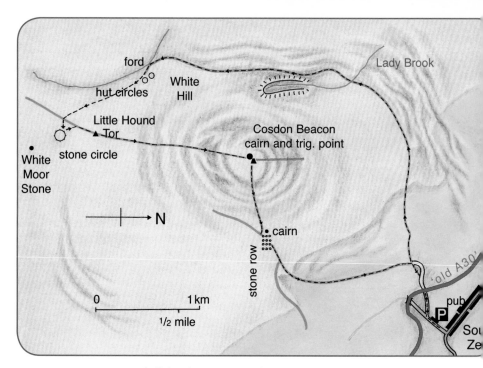

Press on uphill for the MOOR at the next path junction and continue uphill at the next two forks. Go through a gate and up an old drove lane. Keep following the main track to the open moor.

Then keep left twice, in both cases uphill on the stony track. (NB Do not divert south up Cosdon Beacon.) The track now runs parallel to a disused leat, and in time levels out, then descends to cross Lady Brook by a shallow ford. Sheep have created several minor paths.

Stick to the main path, which uses slightly higher ground at a little distance from Lady Brook, and follows the edge of a shallow tin-streaming gulley, then approximately follows the contour along a 'reave' – a long hummock which was once a field boundary.

You should be using your OS map here, but beware: it confidently shows a bridleway to Little Hound Tor but this is not evident as a path on the ground! Check your direction with a compass.

Continue with White Hill on your left, downhill to a ford. Don't cross, but head SE through the heather, passing two hut circles, then gaining height steadily and veering away from the brook and its gulley. Gradually swing from SE to S and press on until you meet the path linking Hound Tor with Little Hound Tor. Turn left along it. The Little Hound Tor stone circle lies just to the east of the track, 400m south of Little Hound Tor, and the White Moor Stone (a Forest boundary marker) lies another 150m from the circle.

14

Walk up to Little Hound Tor and follow the clear path ahead to Cosdon Beacon. This is one of Dartmoor's finest viewpoints: a magnificent array of Dartmoor tors stand south and west, and north and east the rolling hills of mid-Devon lead on to Exmoor.

Turn east at the triangulation pillar, which is perched on top of a massive prehistoric cairn, and follow the path down to the triple stone row. At least 76 stone rows survive on Dartmoor, ranging from a few metres in length to over 3 km. Triple rows are rare.

Stone rows and circles probably date from the Bronze Age, but perhaps even earlier. Their exact purpose is unknown.

The upper end of this triple row is well preserved. A peat track cuts through the middle of the row, and the stones actually extend for a further 60m, but most of them are hidden below the turf. Take the peat track, heading NE.

When the path forks, keep left and follow it downhill between dry stone walls. This sunken track is wet after rain.

Bear right at the next path junction and walk downhill. Continue downhill at the sign A30 AT PROSPECT. Walk on, retracing your steps to Hillfield and back to the car park.

To visit the Oxenham Arms, walk through the car park and bear right into the main street. Turn left.

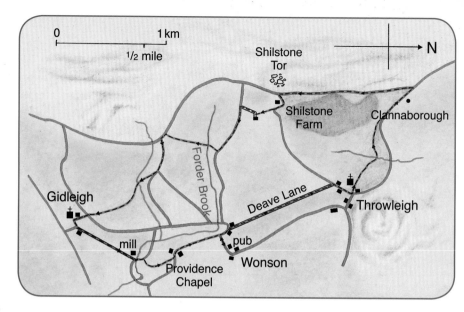

Walk 5 Throwleigh and Gidleigh

Distance: 8.2 km (5 miles)   Time: 2 1/2 hours
Character: This is a gentle walk for all seasons, using quiet paths and lanes. It passes two traditional longhouses, a classic church house, a ruined castle and two fine churches. Parts of the route are wet after rain. The Northmore Arms has customer car parking (01647) 231428.

Park by Throwleigh church (SX 668908). Next to the lychgate is the thatched church house. As well as accommodating the priest, medieval church houses were commonly the venue for parish feasts, at which church ale was drunk. Many later became church house inns.

Follow the path from the west (tower) end of the church through a black kissing gate at the bottom right corner of the churchyard. Walk on through paddocks and over stiles, by PATH signs, then along two sides of a field, with the hedge on your left. Cross a small stone bridge, using the stepping stones over the marshy ground beyond, and up to a narrow gate. Continue through a field.

At the lane, turn left up it. Walk past Clannaborough, a characteristic Dartmoor longhouse. Turn sharp left at the lane junction (SHILSTONE/GIDLEIGH). Turn left again at Shilstone Cross for THROWLEIGH.

Walk by Shilstone Farm, one of the best examples of a Dartmoor longhouse. It began as a single storey medieval hall house, with the farmer's family living in the upper end and their animals below the cross-passage in the shippon. Around 1656, a service wing, decoration and a second floor were added.

Bear right through the gate onto PUBLIC FOOTPATH, to pass Lower Shilstone. On reaching the lane turn left. After 500m, turn right PUBLIC BRIDLEWAY – MARINER'S WAY. Cross Forder Brook by a stone footbridge. Walk on as far as the next lane and turn left.

At Moortown Cross bear left (FORDER/WONSON). When the lane forks after 130m, bear right, then after 150m right again, onto MARINER'S WAY GIDLEIGH. Cross the brook by a footbridge, walk ahead through a gate, and keep the hedge on your right to pass through two more gates. The GIDLEIGH path cuts diagonally across the field to the white arms of a fingerpost. Walk ahead, GIDLEIGH.

On the right is Gidleigh Castle, probably the home of Sir William Prous 700 years ago. Like Throwleigh, Gidleigh church is built of dressed granite (ashlar). It has an excellent carved and painted screen. Turn left at the post-box, across the front of two cottages and down a shady footpath. Turn left at the lane and, 150m ahead, turn right (PROVIDENCE PLACE). Head up the hill to Providence.

At Providence, turn left along the lane and walk past the 1839 Bible Christian Chapel to Barrow Way Cross. Turn right to visit the Northmore Arms, 100m ahead. Throwleigh photographer Chris Chapman's pictures of local life and characters adorn the walls of the inn, which has two open fires and a beer garden.

Retrace your steps to Barrow Way Cross. Turn right, FORDER/ CHAPPLE/GIDLEIGH. By Ivy Cottage, turn right along a track. Follow this pretty byway, known as Deave Lane, to the village, and turn right for your car.

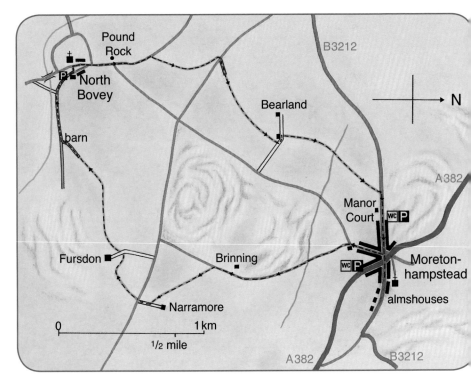

Walk 6 North Bovey and Moretonhampstead

Distance: 7.6 km (4³/₄ miles) Time: 2¹/₄ hours
Character: This walk links one of Devon's prettiest villages with one of its most interesting towns, and passes through attractive farmland by paths and quiet lanes, with views of Dartmoor. It is an ideal route for a winter's day, when short hours and hard weather may forbid longer walks on the high moor – but be prepared for mud.

Start from the car park at North Bovey (SX 740838). Turn right to the village green. This includes a stone cross (once used as a footbridge) and an iron pump. Some of the thatched cottages are 17th century or even earlier.

 Walk uphill from the green. Ignore the first turning on the left but 150 m further on, at Pound Rock, keep left onto a minor lane. After nearly 250 m, look out for a signed public footpath and a stile in the hedge on the right. The route to Moretonhampstead is now indicated by a series of yellow markers – not all equally visible. Cross the field ahead diagonally to a stile and continue to the corner of the next field. Go through two metal gates, turn left and through another gate, then cut across the next field to a stile.

Turn right into the lane and immediately left into a track, PUBLIC
FOOTPATH COUNTY ROAD MORETONHAMPSTEAD. Go through two
gates. Keeping the hedge on your left, and Moretonhampstead ahead
of you, continue on the same course to a farm track. Turn left, then
after 30 m right (PATH).

Follow the waymarks downhill and cross two stiles, to a stream.
Continue, soon uphill by a steeply banked path, to the Postbridge
road – which is often busy: the first short stretch lacks a footway, so
take care. Turn right, passing the Manor Court House, down to
Moretonhampstead's 'Square' – which is triangular, with buildings at
its centre. After taking refreshment at one of the pubs, restaurants or
tea rooms, continue ahead down Cross Street to visit the almshouses
and St Andrew's church. Behind the ashlar front and 1637 datestone
of the almshouses lies a medieval cob building, which was only discovered by archaeologists in recent years. It is thought to have been
the 'hospital' established in 1451.

The church has a splendid 15th century granite tower. In the porch
are two stones with masonic emblems and inscriptions in French to
commemorate two French prisoners-of-war, who died in 1810-11.

Returning to the far corner of The Square, turn first left by the
newsagents for NORTH BOVEY. After 180 m the road forks right for
NORTH BOVEY but you should keep straight ahead, downhill. The lane
crosses a stream and climbs up past Brinning to a stile on the left. Take
this footpath (NORTH BOVEY VIA NARRAMORE & FURSDON), walk ahead

19

across a brook, then two fields, to a drive. Cross over and continue ahead over two more fields. Cross the next small field diagonally to a stile and turn right along the drive.

Cross the lane ahead into the footpath for NORTH BOVEY VIA FURSDON. The route round Fursdon (300 m ahead) is clearly marked via stiles and gates. It continues downhill to a stream and climbs gently, before dipping down to meet a bridlepath beside a stone barn. Turn right and simply follow the path back to North Bovey.

St John's is a granite church, noted for its carved 15th century screen and bench ends. The typically Devonian wagon roof has medieval roof bosses. One depicts the 'tinners' rabbits'. Joined by the ears, these three animals were an emblem of the Dartmoor tinners. Possibly they allude to the Holy Trinity, though some authorities consider they are really hares, and a pre-Christian symbol.

The Ring of Bells (01647) 440375
The building is said to date from the mid 13th century. With its thick granite walls, low ceilings and thatched roof, it has changed remarkably little. The fireplace with its huge bread oven is original too, though the long case clock built into the wall is early 19th century.

The Ring of Bells is thought to have been built as a lodging for stonemasons working on the nearby church; it later became a farmhouse before becoming an inn, possibly five centuries ago. As far as is known, it has always been called by the same name.

Pubs of this name (there are ten in Devon alone) usually celebrate a new peal of bells in a nearby church. St John's had a peal of four bells from medieval times. In 1813 these were melted down and recast as six lighter bells.

Walk 7   From Postbridge to Grey Wethers

Distance: 13 km (8¹/4 miles)   Time: 4¹/2 hours
Character: A challenging walk, unsuitable for inexperienced walkers –
a combination of riverbank paths and open moorland offering
wonderful views. You may share the medieval clapper bridge at the
beginning of the walk with a coach party, but you will almost certainly
have the Bronze Age stone circles of Grey Wethers all to yourself. Parts
of the route are wet underfoot: deep tussocks of grass make for slow and
tiring walking on a 2 km stretch from Sittaford Tor. Avoid rainy periods
and choose a clear day. Boots, map and compass absolutely essential.

East Dart Hotel (01822) 880213
The East Dart Hotel is on the far bank just past the bridge. It began as
a 19th century inn, but became a temperance hotel after the landlady
was convinced of the evils of drink and had the beer barrels emptied
into the river. It regained its licence early in the last century.

   As the attractive new sign of suggests, country sports are very much
the flavour of the hotel. Indeed several local hunts traditionally meet
here and stabling is available for customers. Enquire for fishing, riding
and falconry. Local hunting scenes hang from the walls of the bar,
along with foxes' heads. Enjoy the log fire in winter and the beer garden in summer.

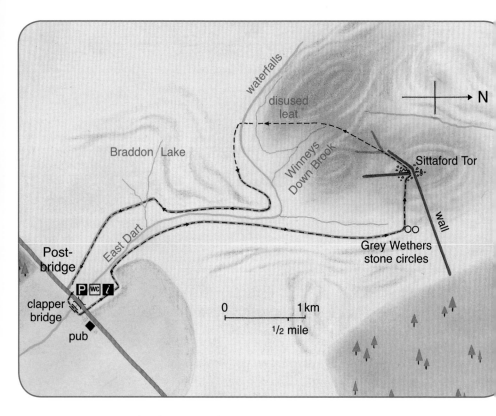

From Postbridge car park (SX 647788) turn left onto the road. Cross the East Dart by the medieval clapper bridge – the largest and best preserved on Dartmoor, alongside the equally handsome 1790 turnpike bridge. Turn left, cross the road and follow the upstream path. This is signed around the edge of the first field, after which it runs parallel to the river. Stick to the contours above the bank to stay dry, and avoid the thicker gorse.

Leave the river when it curves west and head north along a rough path parallel to the brook. In fact there are two serviceable (but not always unmistakable!) paths, one either side of the brook, which later merge on dry ground. Walk on to Grey Wethers, at SX 639831.

A century ago, antiquarians discovered a layer of charcoal at Grey Wethers and at four other Dartmoor stone circles. They concluded that fire played a significant part in the ceremonies performed here. Also, they re-erected many of the stones, which at Grey Wethers are unusual for being generally large and flat-topped. The two circles seem originally to have had the same diameter, each containing 30 stones.

Walk west, parallel to the stone wall, up to Sittaford Tor. At 538 m this is a superb viewpoint. Cross a stile just to the right of the tor and follow the line of the decayed wall ahead, SW for 400 m, at which point the wall apparently peters out. There seem to be paths, but they are unreliable. You need to head SSW, picking your way carefully across tussocky ground (it would be easy to turn an ankle) which can also be waterlogged in places.

After about 800 m (though it will feel like more) cross the head of Winney's Down Brook. Turn south along the gently contoured shoulder of the hill to your right. A disused leat runs around the base of this hill. Cross it and head downhill to meet the river again, beside a charming series of waterfalls.

Cross by the boulders and turn left, downstream. The footing is uneven at first, but soon becomes a real path, which gets much easier once the path bends south, following the contour above the river. At Braddon Lake ('lake' is Devon dialect for a stream) follow the path as it curves away from the East Dart. Cross the stile ahead and turn left, following the path parallel to the stone wall. Cross two small streams.

After 750 m go through a gate and continue back to the car park.

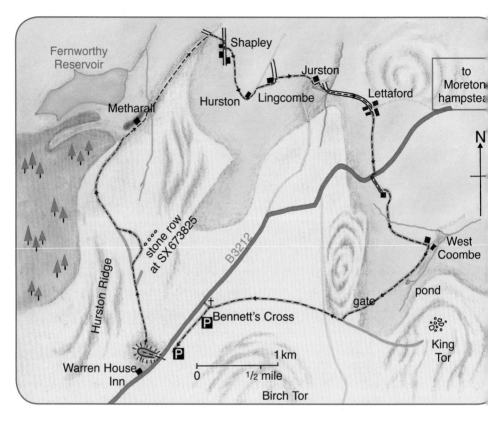

Walk 8   Warren House Inn, Lettaford and West Coombe

Distance: 14.2 km (9 miles)   Time: 4³/4 hours
Character: A mixture of open moor and field paths, this superb walk
has lovely views and much of interest including a prehistoric stone row,
several longhouses and two ancient crosses. One long ascent towards the
end of the walk, one tricky stile. Map and compass essential.

Use the car park just to the east of the Warren House Inn (SX 676812),
called the King's Oven – a reference to medieval tin smelting. Cross
the road and walk up the steep gulley opposite: this is one of many
mining scars in this intensely worked area.

When a rough path crosses the gulley near its upper end, bear right.
The path gradually gains height as it heads to the Hurston ridge.
Ignore cross paths. Keep left at the first fork in the path, then right at
the next, and hopefully you will spot the stone row to your right.

Rejoin the main path and aim for the far north-east corner of
Fernworthy Forest's boundary wall. The paths can be indistinct: if in
doubt, head NNW to pick up the wall, and follow it along.

24

On reaching the lane, turn right along it. Follow the lane past Metherall and then for another 1.3 km to a cattle grid. After a further 70 m, opposite the entrance to Yardworthy, turn right onto FOOTPATH, climbing steep stone steps forming a stile.

Follow the field edge. Turn right at the next PUBLIC FOOTPATH sign along a track. After 150 m turn left at PATH sign. Pass through a small orchard, cross the stile and turn right as signed. Continue through a series of small fields to Hurston. Turn left across the front of the attractive granite and thatch farmhouse. Follow the lane for 230 m, then turn right MARINER'S WAY JURSTON. This is part of an ancient cross-country route used by sailors travelling between Bideford and Dartmouth.

Cross two small footbridges and turn left over a stile. Cross another wooden footbridge, pass Lingcombe farmhouse and immediately turn left, then turn right on PUBLIC FOOTPATH, through fields, heading east to Jurston. Reaching a lane, turn left along it and after 50 m turn right onto MARINER'S WAY MOORGATE. Cross the brook and continue along the trackway to Lettaford, a typical Dartmoor medieval hamlet, originally of three longhouses. In a longhouse, the farmer's family lived at the upper end and the animals at the lower end, in the shippon below the cross passage.

The MARINER'S WAY continues via yellow spot waymarks to the Moretonhampstead road. Cross over and walk on (MARINER'S WAY NATSWORTHY GATE). Leeper Cross is tucked away on the right of the five-barred gate. Follow MARINER'S WAY signs around Moor Gate and then onward to WEST COOMBE. Here the path leads through the farmyard to the magnificent longhouse. Divert 50 m down the lane to see the ash house: it is a circular granite building with a turf roof which was used to store household ash for fertilizer.

Retrace your steps, passing the longhouse on your left. Continue steeply uphill on the bridlepath signed KING'S BARROW. When the concrete path turns right, walk ahead as signed. Keeping the stream on your left, after a while you will pass old mine workings, including a pond. Continue up the well beaten path through the bracken – or in winter, if the path is unclear, head for a gate on the skyline.

From the gate take the minor path (grandly known as the Two Moors Way) which heads west over the brow of the hill and descends to a lane. Cross and continue on the well beaten path over the brow of the next hill, descending to medieval Bennett's Cross. Follow the path through the heather and parallel to the road, to the Warren House Inn.

Sanders, Lettaford

Birch Tor and Challacombe Down in winter, seen from Bennett's Cross

The Warren House Inn (01822 880208)

At 434 m (1425 ft) above sea level, the Warren House Inn is the third highest in England. It was built in 1845, replacing the New Inn, which had stood on the opposite side of the road since it was turnpiked in the 1770s. Its name comes from the nearby rabbit warrens, dug to keep local tin miners in fresh meat. The sign depicts the 'three rabbits', a motif found in Widecombe church and elsewhere in the area and erroneously called the 'tinners' rabbits'. According to Tom Greeves and Elizabeth Stanbrook in their book about the inn, the animals are hares and a pre-Christian fertility symbol.

The Warren House is famous for its open fire, which used to burn 'vags' (peat turfs) and now consumes 40-50 tons of logs per year. It is said never to have gone out.

Walk 9 Lustleigh and the Cleave

Distance: 9.25 km (5³/₄ miles)   Time: 3 hours
Character: A woodland walk, starting at the pretty cob and thatch
village of Lustleigh and exploring both banks of the River Bovey, as well
as its tributary the Becka Brook. We cross the Bovey by a packhorse
bridge and re-cross by huge tumbled boulders. Parts of the route are
steep and can be muddy and slippery after rain. A delightful shady
walk for a hot day.

The Cleave Hotel (01647 277223)

The 15th century Cleave Hotel derives its name from Lustleigh Cleave,
which comes from the Old English *clif*, a cliff or bank. It was originally the main building of Lustleigh Farm, becoming a hotel in the
1920s. The splendid fireplace with its oak beam and bread oven was
discovered in the 1950s. Both bars have log fires and the flower-filled
beer garden is a delight. In the hall there is a good collection of period
photographs, including Lustleigh Station and Lustleigh May Day.

Park in the centre of Lustleigh (SX 785813). Facing the Post Office,
turn left towards BAPTIST CHURCH. Cross a small bridge and walk
ahead for RUDGE. Ignore side turnings and at Rudge Cross walk ahead

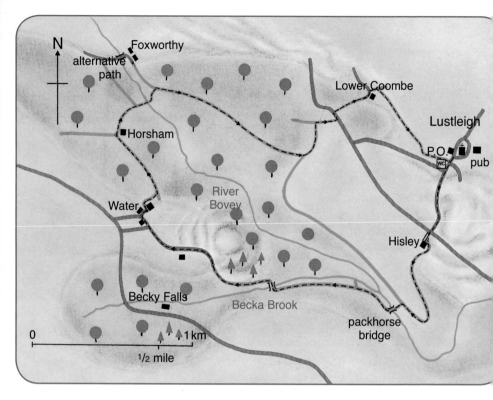

PUBLIC BRIDLEPATH BOVEY VALLEY. Follow the path around Hisley and into the valley, where recent felling has opened out good views over Trendlebere Down. The path doglegs right.

Walk on down, then take the second track on the left to meet the river at Hisley Bridge. A typical Dartmoor packhorse bridge, it is just wide enough for the strings of packhorses that served moorland villages and industries before wheeled transport came into use here in the late eighteenth century.

Cross the bridge and walk ahead to a five-barred gate. Turn right, MANATON. At the next path junction do not cross the wooden bridge: walk ahead, MANATON. Cross the Becka Brook at the next (stone) bridge and go through a gate marked WOODLAND TRUST – WELCOME. Here the Woodland Trust is currently felling conifers of low habitat value to encourage native trees to regenerate. Follow the track up to a junction with a PATH sign.

Walk on uphill on the main track, climbing steeply and ignoring side turnings. Continue ahead at the next path junction, BYWAY TO WATER FOR MANATON.

The path ultimately levels off and becomes a lane. When the lane divides, either divert left for refreshments at the Kestor Inn, or bear right, BOVEY VALLEY FOR LUSTLEIGH. Reaching Water Mill, turn left along the bridlepath. Turn left at the next junction, signed MANATON (INDIRECT) AND HORSHAM FOR FOOTPATH LUSTLEIGH CLEAVE. Ignore side turnings and follow the path past Horsham, following a series of signs for HORSHAM STEPS. Descend into the valley.

Cross the mossed boulders at Horsham Steps *with care*, especially after rain. (For an easier but longer way round by Foxworthy bridge, see sketch map.) Follow the yellow waymarked path upstream along the bank, then right to a path junction. Turn right, HAMMERSLAKE FOR LUSTLEIGH. The path climbs gently to a small fork: keep right with the PATH sign. Turn left at the next path junction for HAMMERSLAKE.

Turn right through a gate at the next fingerpost. Reaching a lane, turn left and after 25 m turn right, CHURCH STEPS FOR LUSTLEIGH. Follow the pleasant woodland path to Lower Coombe. Turn right through a gate for LUSTLEIGH. Ignore the next kissing gate and its side turning. Turn right at the next fingerpost after that (LUSTLEIGH VILLAGE INDIRECT) and take the downhill path. Turn left at the next gate and follow the brook, then cross it by a bridge of boulders and keep left at a path crossing.

Walk on to enter Lustleigh Orchard by a small gate. Continue past the May Queen's throne and the playground to the village centre.

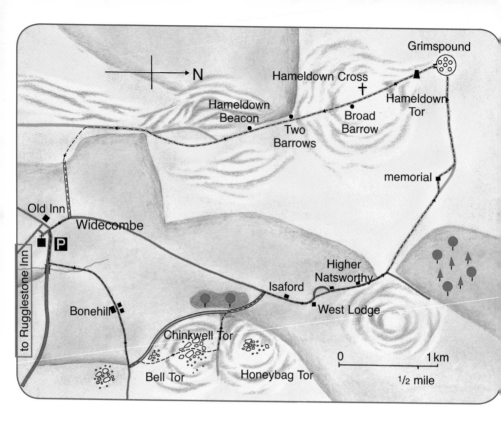

Walk 10 Widecombe and Hameldown

Distance: 12.5 km (7³/₄ miles)   Time: 4¹/₄ hours
*Character: This exhilarating circuit offers some of Dartmoor's finest
views, especially from Hameldown (529 m above sea level). Be prepared
for some steep slopes, especially at the start. A Bronze Age walled village
with hut circles, medieval tin workings, mementos of the Second World
War and a characteristic longhouse add to the interest. High ground, so
map and compass needed for safety.*
Pubs: The Rugglestone (01364) 621327; the Old Inn (01364) 621207.

Park in the car park opposite the church at Widecombe (SX719769).
Turn left out of the car park and follow the BOVEY TRACEY road for
200 m. Just before the bridge over the East Webburn River, turn left
into a lane. This soon climbs sharply and passes Middle Bonehill, a
sturdy granite and thatch longhouse dated 1683 on the lintel.

Continue steadily uphill. Emerging onto the open moor (where
there's a steep hill sign, in case you hadn't noticed it was steep!), turn
left onto a farm access track and 50 m ahead bear right up the steep
flank of Bell Tor. Widecombe's tall church tower appears a mere toy in

30

the valley below. It is dwarfed by Hameldown, russet with bracken in winter, purple with heather in late summer.

Keep to the right of Bell Tor, then head to the summit of Chinkwell Tor and two modern cairns – though one is built on top of an ancient cairn. Now follow the well-defined track down to the col between Chinkwell and Honeybag Tors. Turn left and downhill, following the path down to a track. Turn right and follow the track round and down to a metalled lane.

Turn right and follow the lane past Isaford and West Lodge. After another 200m, use the PATH on the right to cut out a dog-leg in the lane. Walk on and pass Higher Natsworthy Farm, then after another 400m turn left onto PUBLIC BRIDLEPATH ROAD NEAR FIRTH BRIDGE. Follow the broad path uphill, keeping the dry stone wall on your right. Stick to the path as it diverges to the left of the wall, and heads NW.

Just short of the summit is a granite memorial to four RAF crew, killed here when their bomber crashed in 1941. Turn right at the memorial, and then left onto a second broad path which leads over the brow of the hill and down to Grimspound.

This Bronze Age walled settlement covers 1.6 hectares and contains 24 restored hut circles, giving a vivid idea of the size and shape of our

The Rugglestone Inn

ancestors' houses. Distinctly defined on the hillside opposite are medieval tin workings and ancient field patterns.

Leave the settlement by the great gateway on the southern (uphill) side and take the path which climbs up to a triangulation pillar and cairn on Hameldown Tor. Continue ahead on the superb ridgeway track past Hameldown Cross, Broad Barrow, Two Barrows and 'Hamilton Beacon'. Wonderful views of Honeybag, Chinkwell, Hay Tor and Rippon Tor open out.

Keep left where the track forks and follow it down to the corner of a stone wall. Walk ahead (TO WIDECOMBE) with the wall on your left. After 400 m bear left and follow the PATH sign, downhill and into an enclosed track, then a tarmac lane. Turn right at the T-junction, into Widecombe.

For the car park turn left. For the Old Inn turn right. Said to be 14th century and an inn since it was first built, it has been altered and added to over the years. However it retains three good stone fireplaces. There are oil paintings and period photographs of Widecombe. Enjoy the beer garden and the sun lounge in the summer.

Opposite the Old Inn is the 16th century Church House, which includes a National Trust shop (Dartmoor books upstairs) and information centre. It is distinguished by its granite ashlar and its loggia.

To reach the RUGGLESTONE INN, cross the square and turn left. It is 1 km away and can be reached on foot or by car. This small, friendly, locals' inn now offers food all day. Note the photographs of Widecombe Fair and the local hunt, and the 'vagging iron' for cutting peat turfs. Again, there are open fires and a good garden.